HANGING THE ANGELS

Blake Lynch

Finishing Line Press
Georgetown, Kentucky

To Charlie and Jessie

Copyright © 2025 by Blake Lynch
ISBN 979-8-88838-980-5 First Edition
All rights reserved under International and Pan-American Copyright Conventions. No part of this book may be reproduced in any manner whatsoever without written permission from the publisher, except in the case of brief quotations embodied in critical articles and reviews.

Publisher: Leah Huete de Maines
Editor: Christen Kincaid
Cover Art: AJ Weber
Author Photo: Jessie Rose Beard Lynch
Cover Design: Elizabeth Maines McCleavy

Order online: www.finishinglinepress.com
also available on amazon.com

Author inquiries and mail orders:
Finishing Line Press
PO Box 1626
Georgetown, Kentucky 40324
USA

VOICE KEY

The four symbols (✶, ❖, ⊕, ∘) mark the voices of four characters:

Two women. Two men.
Two young. Two old.
Two hold on; two let go.

In my notes, I call them:

        ✶   -   THE THORN-FARMER

        ❖   -   THE WANDERING MARE

        ⊕   -   ADAM

        ∘   -   EVE

You may know them by other names.

Contents

Her Horn
The Wooden Angel / 1
Leaving Gateway Station / 4
Back to Toledo / 5
A Blue Dress / 6
The Losing Kind / 9

Her Hair
The Blew Light / 11
A Rusted Wagon Wheel Outside the Window / 13
Ghosts of the Bramble Slats / 15
To a Friend, Who After Being Diagnosed with Testicular Cancer
Bought a Motorcycle to Race the Wind / 17
Not Praying Outside a Church in Memphis / 19
The Dark Flat Land / 20
Red Star Runner 6 / 22
Private Archipelago / 23

Her Eyes
Rowboat Dream / 25
Mt. Washington Saturday Night / 28
The Moon Is a Motherless Child / 29
Route 22 / 30
The Miracle Never Comes / 31
Every House Light Forgotten, Left On / 32
Fields Go Brown / 33
A Year in Exile / 35
Gone for a While / 36

Her Dress

Dancing with Strangers / 38
Night Cap / 40
A Homestead Grays Jersey Waiting / 41
On Your Knees / 43
Lost Love Is a Honda Door Left Open / 44
A Love Lock for the Hot Metal Bridge / 45
The Wandering Mare / 47
The Fire Doesn't Care / 49
A Stone / 51

Her Feet

Leaving Edith Street / 53
Wildwood, New Jersey / 55
I'll Go On / 56
A Broken Headlight / 58
The Rain Horses / 59
I Never Went to Saskatoon / 61
The 18th Street Stairs / 63
A Road Map for 35 / 64

Her Back

Carry that Weight / 66
Christmas in Budapest / 68
Lodestar / 70
The Hard Swing / 72
The Ghost of the Grape Farmer / 74
Saints and Cannons / 75
Like a Country You Must Leave / 77
Stumbling Off Bigham (Not Eden) / 78

Her Wings

Ditch Flowers / 80

Her Horn

PELUSO–LYNCH ENGAGEMENT NEWS

"Mr. and Mrs. John Peluso announce the engagement of their daughter, Josephine A. Peluso, to Francis Lynch, son of Mr. and Mrs. Bernard Lynch. Miss Peluso is a graduate of the New Castle Hospital School of Nursing. Mr. Lynch is attending New Castle Business College and is employed at the Johnson Bronze Company."

—*The New Castle News,* June 1949

THE WOODEN ANGEL

No one knows where she came from,
but the wooden angel followed me all my life.
It's not only her bare feet,
not the hair tied behind her face,
not her black eyes on the horn,
ready for the fire or the flood,
but the swell beneath her patched dress,
where her wings join her back.

She flies back to 1969.

Grandpa leaves home when the stars
are Irishmen far from Killarney.
Abandoning three faded Arrow shirts,
still buttoned, in a Hazelcroft closet.
He starts a new family. Leaves again.
Grandpa's no river. He moves anyway.

He never knew what he loved.

The day my father's turn comes
to leave Kings Chapel Road,
he drops her in a clothes basket,

in the backseat,
drives off.

He always said it, proud:

> *The day it ended, I just left*
> *with what little I could fit in the car.*

He never knew what he loved.

◆

Between my birth and my father's leaving,
my mother bought the angel.
Vivienne's. Maybe a store in Canfield.
My mother can't remember.

In the division of property,
the angel wasn't worth
fighting over.

She doesn't fly, just moves.

In the angel's black eyes
lived an unclaimed wishbone promise.

My father buried her
at the back of his bookshelf,
behind a stack of Baldaccis.
He never took a hammer.
She never hung on a wall.

o

Say goodbye

driving home under the salt moon.
Cold hands on the wheel.
Don't waste autumn
staring at your shoes.

Say goodbye

humming *Peggy-O*,
Goodbye broken glass.
Goodbye $35.

Write if you can.

From Luzerne to Lawrence County,
we laid our bodies down.

Leaving Gateway Station

Lonely Planet falls from her lap
as she peers through blackout shades,
watching trains leave Gateway Station.
A pigeon dive-bombs the drainpipe,
scaring my hand off a Rolling Rock.

                                    Below, the Three Rivers fork
                                          like a copperhead's tail.
                                  We drink, staring at the water.
                              The Allegheny retreats from its banks.

                                    The river doesn't have
                                even enough water for itself.

                                        Pittsburgh's waiting for the next rain
                                        to wash the Golden Triangle away.

I show her the place silence marked:

    almost visible under my ribs,
    a rail tie called a heart.

I'm following
a thousand things left behind:
a coat left in a law school locker,
long-stemmed flowers in a back seat,
a box of free Neil Diamond records.

Back To Toledo

⊕

If there's luck left on I-69,
after the driver turns the bus back toward Toledo,
when the woman in the first row screams
she'll blow up the midnight bus to Tulsa,
it's that the possum freezing in high beams
isn't crushed under the wheels.

When Leonard, with a missing incisor,
drove her across the border to Pennington,
checking the rearview every six miles,
she almost forgot her duffel bag
stitched together with duct tape,
shoelaces, and prayers.

On the way back to Emerald Avenue,
she pictures her basketball coach
swaying in alfalfa fields,
but that was Mobile, not Indiana,
where he taught her
how to stand still in unguarded spaces.

Now, with everyone watching,
the woman becomes a girl again.
Stanyon Street and Other Sorrows
sticking out of her duffel bag.

> *Everyone you love*
> *meets you at the end,*
> *somewhere between*
> *the old DMV*
> *and the shuttered Metcalf airstrip.*

A Blue Dress

The last time I saw Elizabeth,
she tried her best
to foxtrot past February.

Striped socks.
A side-tied hospital gown.
The rug near the window
became a ballroom.

Elizabeth wished for

> *ruby slippers,*
> *a glass carriage,*
> *a twelve-piece band.*

We danced like they did
in Memphis, after Elvis.

Then, the night nurse came early
to lead her
back to her room.

The sky went grapefruit-pink,
before smoke filtered the stars.

Through winter,
the fern reaches toward
the radio playing Bill Evans.

After sunset, Elizabeth lies still on a table.

She does not float.
She lets her hands fall.
Palms open.
The needle comes.
She tenses.

Her eyes
still as water
after a stone falls.

Out the acupuncturist's window,
Elizabeth saw
how small
the Mexican War Streets were.

An old ring.
A torn picture.
A baptismal certificate.
A tin of saltines.
An angel from the Christmas tree.

Elizabeth still lives in a house in Bellevue.
Clothes flapping in the wind.
I watched her die without realizing it.

My knees were bruised.
I left on a Saturday.

> *I want to marry Elizabeth in a blue dress.*

That night, I wake,
certain there's a fire
burning in the distance.

Elizabeth stands against the dresser,
unfastening her blue dress.

She runs her hands over my hips,
dreaming of reincarnation:
an electric eel,
swimming in the Orinoco River,
charged by her own body,
shocking
anyone who touches her.

◆

The bird we call Grace
flaps in my chest,
burns,
lifts her feathers.

Singing:

> *We're broken bottles.*
> *Still standing.*
> *We go on and on.*

Elizabeth's sleeping in the borrowed chair.
Feet jutting past the ottoman.

The Losing Kind

Emmett

I carry a board
in my rusted Ram.
Stand, alone,
over a fallen colt
in the black field.

Get up, you shitkicker.

Like my no-good ex-wife
I caught in Tinley Town.

I reach for my Case knife
to stab it dead,
but the colt stirs.

Night comes across the pond.
Too dark to see your hands.

I give up,
walk the half-mile home,
under the fading light
of Jackson Public Works
to a house where no one's waiting.

Dave

I'm a tub-and-toilet delivery man
for Brewster's, off Mahoning Avenue.

If the boss needs me in Manhattan at 3 a.m.,
to move his son, kicked out again,
give me two Pepsis, a pack of Reds, and I'll go.

Some nights, I name the stray stars.
They don't know.

The world's not rotating. It's wobbling now.

No one else has ridden these nights on I-78,
hauling a flock of fiberglass tubs.

God said nothing about living like this.

Her Hair

"I walk, sometimes stumble, through this world with my eyes open, recording as much as I can for those who come after. I'm part of a very strange group. If I'd been born at any other time in history, I'd be dead right now."

— *Nine Years Out,* June 24, 2024

The Blew Light

After the first night of chemo,
watching late night reruns
of the *George Lopez Show.*
I said goodbye:

> *to manual windows,*
> *to a parrot fish endlessly circling,*
> *to a banana tree slowly browning,*
> *to Dad and Mary Ann who left.*

In the parking garage,
Dad said:

> *Place the ticket*
> *below*
> *the blue light.*

Mary Ann blew air against the sensor,
hoping the lift gate would open.

Forgive me for laughing at my aunt.
The blue light wasn't for blowing.

I never found Jesus
the way a Houston lunch lady
saw the Virgin Mary
in a greasy pizza pan.
Just busted stars
over a stranger's street.

Tired of watching the Pirates strand runners,
I thought of Vonnegut,
in *Slaughterhouse-Five*,
who found the great pity wasn't Dresden,
but poor Edgar Derby,
shot for a stolen teapot.

> *Cancer became a teapot.*
> *Backed down.*
> *Became hilarious.*
> *Almost manageable.*

The second week,
Mary Ann came every day.
Her brother died at 47.
She called him Johnny.

All day we watched two women
arguing on Court TV
over a Hoover.
I sided with the defendant.
She'd inherited it,
repaired it twice.
She loved that vacuum.
Judge Judy let her keep it.
I won't mention
the woman who lost her dog.

Didn't we deserve to laugh?

A Rusted Wagon Wheel Outside The Window

The rusted wagon wheel,
already wore ice crystals
when I blacked out,
going to the bathroom
and landed on the tile.

At first,
I saw only the darkness.

o

In July afternoon light,
a long way from Luzerne County,
we meet in a clearing.

The only visitor:
a sapling by the river,
arms split open.
Meet me there
when you leave Eastbrook or Virginia
weighing no more than when you came.

You'd have been
a thimble on your mother's finger.

Her Singer's electric now.

I learned to float,
listening in my head
to the holy ghost of Albert Ayler,
playing his horn until it

      shatters,
      shakes,
      screams,

hovers over the audience,
scaring himself and the crowd.

The living fear life:
bird flu,
the Eaton fires,
mass deportation.

A girl in high school called me:

> *Walking dead kid.*

I did nothing.
Today I'd laugh.
I couldn't dance then.

Ghosts Of The Bramble Slats

The winter I arrived
she lived on the second floor,
a jagged shard for a mirror.
We fell in love sharing scars.

°

This is my body.
It's ugly, but I love it.

Stained, torn carpet,
a half kitchen, half dining room,
a bathroom without a tub,
lying on a stained mattress,
slats beneath broken,
we waited for the bulb to explode.

I woke to an infuser beeping.
There was a board on the window,
but I never saw a workman.
She spent all night in the chair,
running her hand over my bald head.
She leaves before dawn,
rides back to California Avenue.

            We were barbed wire.
    Taught to love like strangers
                were watching.

        *The Monongahela River
            didn't save us.*

She sat huddled
at the corner
of the incline car.
Clutching a ride token
in fingerless gloves,
laughing
at the rotting floors.

To A Friend, Who After Being Diagnosed With Testicular Cancer Bought A Motorcycle To Race The Wind

Before my gut was cleaved in two,
I wrote my obituary,
looking at the Neshannock Creek.

I know why you buy a second-hand Harley,
lean into the curve,
not knowing if you'll return.

You want to ride past:
the handkerchiefs doused
in Vicks VapoRub
and Calvin Klein perfume
to avoid smelling citrus cleaner,
but soft rain that keeps returning.

After the wristband,
a spinal needle,
a pain pump,
the mirror shows
a thunderbolt scar,
one stone.

Sometimes only the engine
keeps us breathing.

Might as well dance.
Might as well sing in the dark.
Throw our throttle open
into the coal-black wind.
Call it ours.

Say:

> *This is me.*
> *This is all I carried.*
> *This is all I am.*

When I had nothing,
I lived in frost fields.
I went anywhere.

Keep riding,
you son, brother,
lover, dust rider.

Listen
until the wind
lets you go.

Not Praying Outside A Church In Memphis

Each morning, before I was ready,
I staggered toward a city called Hope.
Not the town my ancestors left,
but where pain was a lost cousin.

I went to Memphis,
but didn't pray at the church
Elvis loved on East Trigg.

I sat in the Jefferson Hotel
reading in today's paper:
a woman on Crump Street
depressed,
rejected,
after catching her man
buying a ring for another,
poured out the Old Crow,
struck a match
to the jug of turpentine,
left the black cat bone
under the porch swing,
and burned her house down.

She let loose the bird
trapped in her ribs.

> *Call it pain, or grief.*
> *Was it sweet like a robin?*
> *Or rough like a goose?*
> *Whatever it was, it flew.*

A lone witness to these days,
I'm not a vulture.

> *Not a blue jay, not a crow.*

Just a loon, still wailing
far across the river.

The Dark Flat Land

Doctors removed my father's spleen
while the radio played *Wildfire*.

⊕

                                  We lived among the dust.
                               In the days before the horses,
                                    the world spun too fast.
                                       Now everything is slow.
                                         A ghost came at night,
                                 not bending the yellow grass.

              We dreamt thunder chased the wind,
                      but never caught it.
                      The wind was always
                            further ahead.

                                                  Horses standing
                                             by a north star lake
                                         are all some folks get.

I woke to my father
running his hand through my hair.
He didn't speak,

    but this is what I heard.

                                                        In the end,
                                   we all lie down in darkness,
                                              smiling at
                                         the growing train
                                         of those we loved.
                                               They're already
                                 arranging folding chairs.

You're my son.
I'm your father.

Go now
along the coast,
*through Fairfield Inns
with crooked pictures,*
looking for light.

Red Star Runner 6

Gauze-cinched tight,
bleeding heels,
swollen belly.
I spent all winter without chairs,
lying against a window,
looking out on Edith Street.

Death started blowing leaves,
rattling fences,
scaring dogs,
but I hid in
the wreckage and bone,

You wanted it easy?
This world's a dirt road.
No one gets out clean.

The river's wide and muddy.
You crawl out stinking of septic tanks.
Waste-filled rivers, if you're lucky.
Fish flopping in your tennis shoes.

Survival meant nothing
without a song to throw back.

I was still running hot,
through the storm,
a woman digging into my ribs.

I floored it
      as lonely as a Red Star Runner 6.

Private Archipelago

One day, you'll forget this version of yourself,
heart like a bruised apple.
You marked the house where you were born
as a place you couldn't forget.
You don't need a speedometer.
You're not going anywhere.
Someday, you'll be me tonight.

Still, I move.

Dan died at 32, carcinoma.
He sat by a quiet creek, waiting.

We're like the passengers
who crashed in the Hudson,
swimming to torn-off wings,
fuselage,
seat cushions,

> *We were blessed by the wreckage,*
> *emerged harder, gentler too.*

My father drove
to Ohio for illegal fireworks.
Bought them from a swamp shack.
They came from nothing, returned to it.

I pray

> *to Quaker Falls,*
> *to the CSX train rumbling at 2 AM,*
> *to Charlie the cat*
> *fed fluid through tubes.*
> *I pray for Dan too.*

I imagine Dan wanted to go,
south to Mexico, just once,
but he was racing the clock.

Dan died seven years ago.
Dan knew.
He smiled.
He made peace with the dark.

      Past midnight at the Menger Hotel.
         I go to the lobby
       to meet the delivery man.
       My husband's knees are sore.
         We're packing shells.

*   Later, if needed,*
we'll return to the empty rockets.

I remember counting lights
beyond the far hill.
The radio screaming:

* Your papa's done got a gun.*

One day,
it'll be
too late
to be anything
in this strange light.

What no one tells you
about aging
is you're mostly fine with it.

You become an old house alcove.
When it rains, the whole street leans in.
Not just kids and parents.
Strangers too.

Some nights, that's enough.

Her Eyes

"I envy religious people. When people die, they believe it means something. But I just don't. When people die, they just die. Nothing other than that."

—Anonymous, *Ghosts of the Last Light*, March 20th, 2020

Rowboat Dream

o

March came, flowers blooming
like a woman's gray hair.

The virus came.
We lived in it
like jarred grasshoppers.

They said the only treatment
was an anti-malarial.

I took the chloroquine
forgotten in the shed.
Half an hour: throwing up.
Then fever. I dreamt:

>*Magellan, alone in a boat,*
>*staring into nothing.*
>*He didn't know what to call it,*
>*so he wept anaconda tears.*
>
>*The rowboat carried a ladder*
>*nailed to the sky.*
>*We told him: Paint the wind.*
>*Gave him half the rungs.*
>*He didn't climb.*
>*Just sat, wounded.*

*Goodbye, Ferdinand.
We're headed
back to Spain.*

*Goodbye
blue-lipped crowd
outside the Pittsburgh Zoo,
waiting for tests.*

*Goodbye, flat blue hills,
river trout,
coyotes.*

We'll never see you again.

⊕

I drove four hours on 376 for a test.
Parked in a ditch
before the toll booth.

Lights off. Doors locked.
I didn't have a dollar.

Norman, the night worker,
let me walk into town
to get what I needed
from a humming box of light.

The aisles were
pink cakes,
Monster cans.
Nothing
in the empty night.

*I was a skunk
that doesn't survive winter.*

Doesn't the thought
you can dump your car
by the side of the road
then spend the rest of your life walking

seem so freeing,
it could break your heart?

Mt. Washington Saturday Night

✦

Chain-smoking Camels,
waiting for the Powerball,
Ed's hair is long and dirty
like Uriah the Hittite,
but Ed can't flee to Egypt,
only a secondhand La-Z-Boy.

Gunsmoke mutters
from the corner Magnavox.
He pounds a Natty Lite,
wrists curled with pain and beer.

It rained so hard
off Grandview last night,
Ed swears a twister'll come,
rip out the chain-link fence,
level the house.

> Once, I rode all night
> to Baltimore and back
> to buy my new dog, Zoltan.
> Window down,
> a leaf slapped me.
> I swear it was my dead grandmother,
> whacking me
> like I was sixteen
> sipping her whiskey
> and filling it with water.
>
> Memory's not a twister tonight.
> What we remember's quieter:
>
> *a wolf in the distance,*
> *nose full of diesel fumes,*
> *out hunting.*

The Moon Is A Motherless Child

Travis

All day, I painted McTavish's barn blue.
By dusk, he wanted it green again.

I wanted to dig where stars go
when they've burned out,
but went back alone to my trailer
off Route 79, Jackson exit.

Arms sore from Gildan cans.
My hand still periwinkle.
Headlights beaming across the wall.
Candy took the fish tank too.

I stand in the yard,
looking through the fog,
waiting for the cat statue
with a fishing pole
to bring the ending
wished for in the dark.

We were Bucks Family scratchers,
left on the table for days.
Scratch with a counter penny.
Lose again.

I bought a second kitchen chair.
Sanded and painted it.
No one sits there.

The moon floats, bare,
above the toilet flower planter.
Never finds others like it.
At least, the moon never wonders
if its mother had blue or green eyes.

I do.

ROUTE 22

Her white scarf floats
down behind her
like the tuna cans
her fiancé threw away.

Her fingers tug
at her pearlescent necklace,
as if her right hand wants
to give her soul room to escape.

In her note, Evelyn scratched out:

> *I don't think I would make a good wife for anybody.*
> *He is much better off without me.*

Not just better. *Much*.

All she heard was a whir.
Limestone, steel, fog, clouds,
taxis, rooftops, pigeons turning gray.

Her fiancé moved to Florida,
and spent fifty years
talking to himself
in Publix parking lots,
and NASA buildings,
as the country pulled
away from the moon.

An engineer,
his fours were too straight.
Even his numbers all looked sad.

Now she's a light left on Route 22,
but he's dead now, car scrapped.

The Miracle Never Comes

◆

In the last photo
of Andy Kaufman
the light falls uneven
across his shirt.

Maybe I'll fake my death.

The kind of dark joke made
when you're leaving,
like how I wanted
all October, with cancer,
to take my picture
in a stranger's yard
on a stationary bike
beside two skeletons.

Everything outside the picture
already laughed:

a brown truck leaning into the roadbed,
a plane crawling low over rice fields.

o

I was born
in a house with copper pipes
laid by a man I never met.
That's all we are before loss.

Time after,
I learned what every lead joint did.

I sit up until 2 A.M.,
looking back at the pictures left,
laughing at my pain.

The pipes kept running.

Every House Light Forgotten, Left On

I came down,
after the tourists left,
stood at the shoreline,
counted what would wash away.
Dreamed I was the coastline.
I became worn sandals,
the strap falling off.

I left every house light on.

                        Hang up your late-night dues.
                        They're singing one last song.
             One for the devil. One for the blues.
    One for the girl in gladiator shoes.

Framed in the glass door,
my face lit sideways.
I catch my breath.
                Am I really that old?

I never sat by the Hudson,
that brown, dirty river.
No one ever called.

I don't want to exist.
Not a country.
Not a name.

Weekend mornings crawl.
                Another Sunday mourning.

I shut the light off.

Fields Go Brown

✦

Behind her former house
lies a garden overgrown with weeds,
a Tacoma with a rusted license plate,
bent by kids with hammers.

The man who bought the house
lets them visit.

She watches her five-year-old daughter
who loves marigolds and Indianheads,
folds fresh grass into shopping bags.

She wishes her heart were more
than Fletcher's Chapel,
waiting for the abandoned Garrett farmhouse
to fall to splinters,
where the air smells like rotten eggs
because Lorton's dump is full.

Her mother wants
to warn her daughter
if she lingers
she'll be unpicked corn,
or worse,
trapped by a rust knuckle man
who drives a ghosted F-150
with Kid Rock stickers.

He always took her camping.
She hated camping.
He took her to a Super 8
on 29, near Charlottesville.
She sat by the door,
waiting for Domino's.

She forgot:
until she was caught in the grass
at Morris Field on Independence Day
with a strawberry-sized mosquito bite,
and memories of his bowlegs.

                                                  She stares past
the concrete rental yard,
the shanty town of umbrellas
built to stop the rain.
A Queen Anne's lace
blooming in the darkness.
Waiting for wind chimes.

A lone tree still stands
in front of the two-story
where her family lived.
Roots knotted so deep
no grapple could tear them.

She collected pepperweed
and placed them on her rented Maytag,
always wrote thank you cards.
A thrift store-seeker of love.

Miles from the Outer Banks,
she lowered the windows
to smell the ocean and listen.

Your mother, child,
was a satellite dish,
signals gone,
bending in the wind.

A Year In Exile

⚬

I asked if you remembered
our first Christmas,
when I bought you
an ornament of Santa skiing,
like the one your mother bought
in Volant at a country store.

Someday, you promised,
you'd buy me a stocking
with a smiling elf,
and my name stitched on.

I woke the day after Christmas,
in the dark house, in relief.
I squeezed into jeans. Felt old.

The town fathers never built
statues for people like us.
We work night shifts.
Skipped college.

Went to Hooligan's on Saturday nights.
Sat in the corner while the jukebox played
Melvin singing *Just My Imagination.*
You'd take a sip of Wild Turkey,
lift it in the air.
Sing, mostly off.

When you're young,
there's not a shadow's chance.
But we're old,
we drink, we toast.
We're less than perfect.
A fraction of the Holy Ghost.

Gone For A While

Tanya

◆

We laid Daddy down Friday.
It wasn't COVID.
Just bone cancer.

My Brownie niece
sang *Precious Memories*
in the hallway
of Tucker's Funeral Home.

I thought about my Huffy.
I wanted pink streamers.
Never got them.

◆

When he wasn't digging
telephone pole holes,
Daddy was a painter.
He wouldn't paint this.

My husband's out again
with those boys from Kings County.
When this marriage ends,
I want to go fishing again
on the Rappahannock.

My mom never said,

I love you.

I grew up thinking
there was something wrong with me.
She wrote my book reports
while Dad, Lisa, and I were sleeping.

I want to go back
to Kmart blue-light specials.
A broken Iron City Beer clock.
A faded White Snake cassette.
Big Mouth Billy Bass
that danced on the wall.
A red leather Bible
embossed with Tanya.

Jesus. Love let me down.

I miss Tip O'Neill.
People still like to be asked.
I miss the old stuff.
There's no map.

Husbands and mothers
want you
folded like laundry.

No one listens
when you return,
Wranglers stained
black with mulch.

I don't care if they're left waiting.
I'll hang a sign, even.
Leave the light on.

Her Dress

"I have too many of my mother's tendencies."

—Evelyn McHale, 1947

Dancing With Strangers

After a few Sam Adams,
she sinks the 7 ball.
My cousin starts again.
The Akron haze.
Smells like burning tires.

Out here,
we do our best
dancing with strangers.

○

> The last third of your life,
> you're a broken arrow.
> Tip bent,
> you still flew.

I'm a light stain on the Rust Belt.
She's heartbreak
beneath the sign
at Thistletown Racino.

Her hands hurt
from folding clothes
on a double at JCPenney's.
Twin babies
in a one-bedroom.

She sleeps
downstairs
in a sleeping bag
near the furnace.

⊕

In the photo Valerie took,
I'm staring
into a backyard fire bowl.
A Pug snorgling at my feet.

Behind me,
the purple sky ignores
two helicopters,
flying low.

Night Cap

The wind is already blowing
side mirror glass across Gladstone Street.

That winter, she crashes through a fence.
The wires hummed,
almost laughing.

She still carries
the scar on her thigh.

      I couldn't fix it.

Before the lights go out,
your father pours Wild Turkey,
whistling until the sun returns.

      At a Walnut Street parade
      on Memorial Day,
      you take your hand off my shoulder,
      slip past the chain-link fence
      to Needles or Oakland.

      Returning to my father's house,
      my mother gathered fallen avocados,
      left them in Walmart bags
      beside the transistor
      she held onto.

I'll remember later
the knife-bright green of the unripe ones.

A Homestead Grays Jersey Waiting

We sat
in a cracked
Red Robin booth.
She came from the Palouse,
was headed back soon.
Fry oil. Mustard-stained light.
We couldn't stop it.

A framed Josh Gibson jersey
behind glass, sleeves raised
like he still might return to claim it.
Gibson died of a stroke
before we were born
just months before
Jackie broke the color barrier.

                                        We started a little west of Idaho.
                                                              At four,
                          everything still belonged to me:
                                     grandma's floppy hat,
                             the disgruntled lawn mower,
                             the rotary phone I thought
                                            was connected.

I've grown a beard,
stare at the photo.

Your yellow scarf,
soft at the throat.

I'll never throw away
the rain jacket you left.

                                    Losing me?

                                You beat cancer.
                            You're scared of nothing.

                       I kept the dried stalk of wheat
                             you tucked into my copy
                       of Brautigan's *Dreaming of Babylon*.
                           It's brittle now, shredding.

                                I won't let it go.

Sometimes you're like Josh Gibson.
You build frames. Leave them.
That's all.

               The sound of a train in the distance.

On Your Knees

After the cancer wars
came the lean, lean years.
Most nights I drink alone
at a bar on Monterey Street,
$25 burgers served in red baskets
with stale fries.

The lonely waitress
reminds me of no one.
She wipes hard,
like she's scrubbing
sorrow off river rocks
with a bar rag.

The sky falls like ash from a coal fire
onto the old man (could be any man)
beneath a Ryder truck cap,
rarely speaking.

Eve is the stars now,
hanging above the road
on the way back from Wheeling.

Tonight, the dead come
sit beside you, buy you a beer,
until the air outside turns green
with streetlights and fog,
and it's just dark in here.
You crawled through the dark
to find your way back
to that bar by the river,
but you get scared,
end up back on the streets.

Lost Love Is A Honda Door Left Open

Her mother had just died, young.
All that was left
after the fire
were black beams,
overgrown ivy.

Later, they found her dog
on the railroad tracks
headed west
like love
walking off into the night.

I loved her.

I didn't answer.

Because youth
was a cement statue
hurled into the water.
I would've gotten
my shoes
dirty.

Lost love was a Honda door
left open on the shoulder of a gravel road.
I debated shutting it,
leaning my weight against it,
but the hinge was rusted.

A Love Lock For The Hot Metal Bridge

Red, swollen marks
up and down her chest,
like she left her jacket on
after rising from some river.
Eyes like bellflowers.
She holds the blanket
tight to her chest.

                                        Summer's fruit rots too.
                                        God bless the trees
                                              for trying.

I hold a dropped hair band
while she talks
of her father
reading *Song of Songs*,
where a woman
chased her lover
through Jerusalem's dirty rain.

The streets are still dirty.
I don't search the city.
We're already
two phone screens flickering.

                                        After washing my face
                                                  I notice
                                          a penny left
                                      in fireplace brick.

                                        I wish someone
                            would make a lock for me
                              on the Hot Metal Bridge,
                                  but it's heavy now.
                                The city cuts off locks.
                                  Doesn't return them.

If I dwell longer
on what I lost
to get to where I'm headed
the pain will bloom dark purple.

The Wandering Mare

The mare comes,
only when the Homestead train's quiet.
She snores like a hacksaw,
hangs fake ivy in the bathroom window.
As soon as she gets the money,
she'll head back to Jackson.

                                                        Silence.

What do you want?

                                                        Nothing.

Real people run
until they turn to bone.

I patch what I can
with a claw hammer.

I write past dawn
like Hailu Mergia
at the Addis Ababa Hilton.
Only, I'm alone.
There is no danger.
Still, a *tezeta*.

                            I want love like the Allegheny River.
                               The kind that leaves the bed made.

You should've been here last week.

                                                    It must hurt.

Like nothing I know.

She walks to another town
slowly,
believing I'll follow,
under alcoves and alleys,
avoiding the moon.

I don't.

                                              I don't love you.

At 3 a.m., I stand alone,
pick up the fallen screen
that once divided the yards.

        I want a river.
        I have no boat.
        I don't even live by a river.

The Fire Doesn't Care

I hope love finds us
on a slip of paper tied to a pear tree.

The tree couldn't hold that wish,
because love was left
in a fire burning,
fueled by scraps,
a Goodwill desk,
warped record shelves,
a torn chair.
It spread,
indifferent to you or me.

Through boxes,
under paper,
across torn-up
checkerboard floor.

A neighbor in faded flannel
called the cops.
The firemen said
I couldn't burn
what was left
of what I owned.

I let the ashes stay.
I don't sweep the glass
or toss the silver knob
that refused to burn.
I pick up the ribbons
of worn notepads.
Words I've forgotten.
Can't decipher anymore.

I'll never know
what I lost.
The sky won't either.
It all becomes
a ball of black soot.

I rarely walk the quarter mile
down to Carson Street,
past The Club Café,
which nearly burned.
I will tonight,
to buy paper towels
to wipe my hands.

That tree in Pasadena
was likely burned
in another desert fire.

Someday, I'll send her a postcard.

A Stone

The last time on Shiloh Street,
passing the liquor store,
where I dropped *Eddie the Head*
on an Iron Maiden beer
into a thousand pieces.

We never knew,
when we met at Redbeard's,
the end too would come
under a neon pirate sign.

                                      The woman smoking outside The Summit.
                                            Purse heavy with rhinestones.
                                              On it, Mickey Mouse's hands
                                                       frozen mid-air,
                         pointing toward heaven, or just stuck.
                                    A cartoon mouse turned
                                              third-shift dreamer.

Back in Pittsburgh alone.
I sit in the hot tub.

The Duquesne Incline
lights blink a promise
made to watch over her.
My body held on.

Mickey kept pointing.
Robbery or heaven,
I don't know.

For hours,
I stare at the telephone poles,
a rusted shovel leaning
against my neighbor's knee wall.

No one hears, just chlorine.
A jet that doesn't blow.
It knows no heaven.
Only my back.

> *I'm nearly round.*
> *I'm not a stone.*

Her Feet

"Daddy, how far could you run if you had to?"

—Charlie (age 5) 2022

Leaving Edith Street

o

Last time.
Window rolled down,
garbage stacked at the curb.

An old raccoon
tore the bags open,
ate scraps.

Ripped Lou Reed t-shirt,
faded Gutchies.

Under elms,
I tell myself
lies.

I'm
a small brown sparrow,
a rocking chair,
empty lots.

Nothing cares.
We burn down.

> *Leave nothing,*
> *almost something.*

Torn leather,
stuffing spilled out.

Everything promised:
already dust.

We owned nothing.
We rented love.
Returned it.

Wildwood, New Jersey

The Shawnee believed
the dead spoke in wild wood.
Was every gash in the bark
a question?

I wade ankle-deep in the Atlantic,
thinking of those vanished Saturdays.

I wish on the Atlantic for light.
Not to God, but Grace, a woman.
She watches.
I gamble and stagger alone.

There's an Igloo cooler
under the pier.
Muddied white,
the color of her blouse
at that whiskey bar.

On the boardwalk,
beauty comes worn-down,
a carousel horse,
paint peeling off its shoulders.

I hold a dime.
Still warm in my hand.

On one side,
Roosevelt, staring off,
kept the *Houston* on his desk.
It sank in 1942.
He stayed in his chair.
He'd have made a good sailor.

Flip it over.
A torch still burns.
No one tells you
that fire doesn't mean hope.
It means something's burning.

I'll Go On

◆

Tomorrow, I'll drive
to her apartment in Ruckersville, Virginia
with strawberry plants
and *Wildflowers* by Tom Petty
hanging above her bed.

I'll carry the wooden nickel
my father brought from Italy.
I didn't want it.

◆

Madison, full of defeat and Christians.
Someone hung a *Fuck Biden* banner
from the window
over the gun store.

Her mother cried at the wedding,
then danced on yellowed linoleum.
The woods go dark before seven.
Deer run again. It's rutting season.

My father never shot deer.
Once, he brought home
a mallard wrapped in tinfoil.
It flapped in the mud,
then stopped.

When I go, I want
to be like that duck.
Bury me beneath a split tree
in a field no one visits.

✦

My father taught me
to fish the Neshannock Creek,
how to make the lure jump like light.
Tied them by lampglow
with his small red fingers
at an old girl scout camp,
tweezers in one hand,
reading glasses on.

⊕

Like Samuel Beckett after the war,
holding a stone
from a field
somewhere in France.
He picked it
because it asked nothing.

He asked nothing.
Wondered if the river
had kicked the stone loose.

All it had was moss on one side.

No wings. No feathers.

I'm the same.

A Broken Headlight

Kelly lived in Lancelot Trailer Park,
a ten-foot sword out front.
A glass and sand bank,
where a boy I knew
tried to drown his father's body
in a truck locker.

We went to my school's
spring dance.
She only moved
to go to the bathroom.

I don't stop,
just turn up the radio.

I go back to Jackson,
in a car with its headlight
broken by a deer.
The beams dance:
sometimes shining,
sometimes scattering.

After the dance,
we sat in my Jeep.
Engine running.
I asked to kiss her.
She said no.

Kelly, did you ever move away?

If you aren't careful,
you'll end up a tree.
You'll stay thirsty all summer,
finding no water,
only concrete and crushed Budweisers.

I did.

The Rain Horses

I called her Rose,
but she was born Katherine.

She left behind a birthday card,
a morphine bottle, and a Snickers bar.

Now I'm the rain lifting
haloes of steam off
the San Antonio River Walk.

In Memphis, I sat in the car, idling
down the street from the Lorraine Motel.
Martin was struck down
like the lightning bolt
that hit the cross on Miller's Barn.
Everything after was haunted.

Ended up in Handy Park.
The sky
pale as a jawbone.
I became a rain horse,
nothing special,
just lonely in a field.

Uncertain, I ran into
this bruised country's wind
to Bugtussle, Kentucky.

Rose became what she wanted:
a red-winged blackbird,
vanishing down a fire road.

> *Feathers coated with soot*
> *from flying too close to fire.*

I ended up back in Lubbock.
Gazing at the rain,
listening to rusted wheels clatter.

A woman pushing
a three-wheeled shopping cart,
singing:

> *Oh, Susannah.*
> *Don't you cry for me.*

Skimming cold rocks
in Yellow House Draw,
I wish Rose lived
in those rocks that press down
on moss,
on mud,
on catfish,
waiting for better summers.

I Never Went To Saskatoon

✦

Gasoline
or kerosene?
What did those kids
dump on you?

I named you Chance.
The woman in Akron
who sold you for $20
called you Red.

Your sight gone,
you got trapped behind the couch.
Your remains
stayed in a box
on the kitchen counter.

> *Listen, this part's hard.*
> *The caretaker lied.*
> *He dumped you in a landfill.*

Years after you died,
I went to the French Quarter.
I didn't know what else to do.

○

                                          The house we lived in
                                            is so delicate now
                                   you could knock it over
                                      with your memory.

                                                     I held you
                  until you were just a lock of hair.

                              The trees will be trees again.

I'll follow you
out of lonely Pirate Avenue,

Stand still,
so I can look through you.
Guts and bones now.
Aren't you, Thorn-Farmer?
Waiting to be made
whole again.

I'll stay
as long as you need me.

You'll talk to me at night,
when no one else is listening,
with your heart on fire,
naming everything.

The 18th Street Stairs

⊕

If I could come back
as the unfaded
blackbird tattoo
on your wrist,
I wouldn't say a word.

Grandpa Charlie was dead
long before we met,
but I know the song
he sang about the blackbird
on the porch
when you were little.

*I still say your name
on backroads no one remembers.*

After lifting Dobermans at the clinic,
carrying sick cats in for x-rays,
you come home tired.
You don't say a word.

We aren't birds.
This is not heaven.
So I walk
up the ten flights
of 18th Street stairs,
ascending Billy Buck Hill,
leading to sky
and strangers' houses.
I'm the only one
who climbs them.

*Each time, I reach the top,
you're still gone.*

A Road Map For 35

Under that tree outside your window,
we dug for treasures.

Taking the garbage to the dumpster,
you held my hand,
trusting me to show you
how to cross between cars.

I love you like the air that holds back a fire.
My heart is a small flame.
Yours fills every object in the room.
You're the one I'd always choose to save.

I'm the storm.
You're the lighthouse.

I have nothing
but a field of weeds where you can rest.

When you're older,
you might carry everyone you love in pictures.

You'll drive for hours through little towns,
far past Madison,
where joy and sleepless hours
braid together like old roads.

I hope you always believe
the dust hanging in the air
is your dead beagle, Carlson,
reaching down from heaven.

Love, if it's anything,
is a Polaroid
of my mother at twenty-three,
her hair the color of fire
before the sparks.
A chestnut horse
resting its head
on her shoulder.

Luck is a fistful
of uneaten rice
thrown over a campfire
before the rain starts.

Life is an x-ray
of every bone
sprained or broken,
a reminder
of every time
you picked up the rope again,
kept jumping.

Her Back

"He's built his house from bones and rainwater. He's still looking for the river that runs backwards."

—Ellis McRay Barrett, *Hollow-Born: Strange Songs & Border Histories from the Lost South,* 1927

Carry That Weight

After buying a hundred-year-old house,
I knelt and peeled back the Lowe's carpet,
and stared out the window
at the houses across Pius Street:
chimneys, red doors, stacked garbage.

I carry this weight,
past apartment after apartment,
a house I bought and sold,
but even without water,

        I lasted.

I believed the tree
the driveway curled around
in the house where I grew up
had roots worth saving.
I believed in
the oak floors too,
but for years
I left them hidden
under black laminate.
I was afraid to tear it up,
but a month before I sold that house,
I did what I could.
I loved that floor.

One weekend:
heat gun, hammer, chisel.
Wearing a face mask,
I leaned into the peeling,
carried the weight
clean as the big stone
at the end of my grandpa's driveway.

Christmas In Budapest

At fifteen, I slept with a pad and pen
beneath my pillow.
My grandpa asked:

> *How can you see in the dark?*

That year, I wrote a rambling thing
I called *Christmas in Budapest*.
I'd never seen the Danube,
never felt the cold
of a place I couldn't pronounce.

At the boarding school's Croft Dormitory,
nights were locked, undisturbed
like a toolshed drawer in December.
I pulled radio wires across the nights,
building a house I could live in.

I lived with Joe from the Hill district.
We shared a room with cracking walls.
I wasn't there when he left.
I didn't see him again for years.

I was a whisper, then.
I wrote anyway.
I do it now,
tearing rusted screws
from rotted steps,
leaving a hole
the dogs keep leaping,
never clearing.

I still hear Joe saying:

> *Don't let them change your voice.*
> *But I was from the East Hills.*
> *My mom was from the Hill.*

Did I listen enough?

I imagine Dr. Simon too,
who came before dawn and said:

> *No, you damn fool,*
> *it's not going to kill you.*
> *Keep moving.*
> *There's light.*

So I did.

After repairing the steps,
I replace the outlet in the yard,
then go down
into the mud basement,
and flip the circuits back on.

It's Saturday morning
in a house I own.

Lodestar

All evening, the Black girls braid.
Kenekalon lies on the table,
as Elizabeth twirls,
arms lifted to an invisible radio.

> *You love her more than the moon?*
> *The rain?*

The tall one laughs,
not lying as she braids and wraps.

I notice the scar on her shoulder
from jumping out of a Pontiac Sunfire.
She runs a pick through the hair
of the girl cradling a baby from bedsheets.
No one knows where the real one went.
The night nurse takes her up to the roof.

In the corner of the room,
an old woman cracks
vending machine pecans,
thought they were M&Ms.
Nearly blind, she waits
for me to read from *SkyMall*.

She'll visit Tahiti someday.

We don't fly in Western Psych,
but at seventeen, sometimes,
if I leaned just right,
I'd float for a moment toward the North Star.

Melissa, the night nurse, sits at a bolted table,
clutching her dented Aladdin thermos.
Icicles hang from stained glass:

Jesus carrying the lamb no one claimed.
Jesus ate meat.
She likes the empty Sewickley apartment,
but darkness sometimes comes.

Driving home, Melissa thinks of the ditch,
of heading south to Florida.
Let PennDOT decide
if she was raptured or stolen.

> *Melissa comes back the next night,*
> *just stands by the curtains.*

She tells no one.

The Hard Swing

Sonny Stitt recorded over a hundred albums.
Sonny Stitt has been dead for decades.

My heart still paces
outside the Mardi Gras Bar
on Copeland Street,
where the dogwoods shiver.

Whenever they play *I'm Old Fashioned,*
bent sweet and slow,
I worry about getting home,
afraid of falling into the fire,
lit before I was born.

I'll go someday too.

When I do, let there be:

a winter moon,
a record spinning,
a saxophone naming the dead.

This year's fancies are passing fancies.

I should be grateful I survived cancer.

We who remain
are told we must be
fat raindrops
falling off gutters.

I ended up a skip in the groove.
A faded record.

Desire doesn't leave.
It lives
in rain, in air.

I wait for the disease to return,

to turn me into
a small pool of light
for the rest of my life.

When I go, let them say:

>*He lived without hesitation.*
>*He wanted everything.*

So did Sonny Stitt,
but he's long gone.
He's dusk now.

>*I don't mind it.*

He's the window
you can barely see.

That old horn, warbling
like a ticket stub
that fell from my grandfather's blazer
in 1968,
when he visited Chicago.

No one claimed it.
It lay there,
quiet,
until the night janitor found it,

eyes open,
dreaming,
asking:

>*What wreckage of memory*
>*can we bring through the night?*

The Ghost Of The Grape Farmer

This hacking never stops,
late October's reminder
of fear and middle age.
Rising after dark to stillness,
to the sheets I fought all night.
Coughing,
gasping for air.

I go walking after midnight
down Warrington Avenue
and see Larry Levis
standing in the dark
inside *The Thread Closet*.

The son of a grape farmer,
he's not bothered
by the Penguins sweatshirts
and steel hangers.

No. It's just a shop window.

I turn wrong
into Wharton Street alley,
hoping when I emerge it's 1979.

o

                            My father is on his way to meet my mother,
                                          in a green VW Rabbit,
                          the stars strung like volunteer soldiers
                                    lining the Amish lanes,
                                  the one my uncle called
                                          the beard roads.

The longer you carry it,
the more it hollows you.

Saints And Cannons

⊕

That summer, I wore:

A Gonzo pendant,
a silver fist in the air.
It pressed heavy
when I walked.

A Christopher medallion.
My father brought back from Sicily.
Another trip without me.

Christopher was beheaded.
Hunter shot out of a cannon.

At night they pressed
against my chest,
asking:

> *Do you bend for others,*
> *get quietly beheaded*
> *or scream*
> *until the fuse explodes?*

I'm waiting for someone
with a frayed rope
and a clearance Coleman lantern.
But I've always liked fireworks.

I sit in the hot tub,
writing into *The Simple Truth*.
By morning, I couldn't read it.
Phil Levine was just gone one day.

I write until the pen gives out.

Later that summer,
I was cleaning my CZ-75
when it fired into my bedroom's drywall.
No one came. I wasn't arrested.
Instead, I dragged my speakers
out into the little backyard,
playing Lester Young past two.

○

That strange angel wanders the South Side,
watching lit windows.
He rattles my door at night.

Tomorrow, I'll meet him barefoot.
He knows my name.
I don't know what he is,
maybe just something I hope is there.

I gaze out:

row houses,
a torn-off drain pipe,
scraps of checkered tile.

Tonight, I'll sit in the dark.

Like A Country You Must Leave

(If I left before you.)

⊕

You'll live by the highway.
Your red hair, faded.
The cornfields dried out in August.
The wind laying low the weeds.
At night, you'll rise,
naming the fixed stars
like people call their dead.

You'll become water,
slow, stubborn,
slipping through ditches,
looking for a place to vanish.

You'll find only dirt.
You'll drive again.

o

If I'd stayed,
who would I be?

I dream of rabbits with your eyes:
soft-bellied, alert.
You'll be safe
in a field no one cuts,
awake beneath curtains
that never close.

If I lost you,
what would I become?
A country, maybe.
The kind you flee,
fire catching behind you,
the town hall flames
small enough, at first,
to mistake for lanterns.

Stumbling Off Bigham (Not Eden)

She asks why night exists.
I don't know.
Stare out.
Not enough copper
to run the sun all day.

I fall into
her rough laundry hands.

> *I'm sin.*
> *She's sin.*

We're husband and wife.

We walk.
We stop at gates.
Keep going.
Never find sleep.

        I couldn't hear the herons
        when he unsnapped my jeans.

        Now he wanders Virginia.
        Letters in his coat,
        same blue eyes,
        beard gone red.

        This child thinks
        a stork left him.

>   *I'll break*
>   *before I bend.*

✶

I fled
on a flat tire.

Yellow gas light
blinking low.

Suitcase thrown
in the backseat.

I fled.

                                                               ○

                                               Hide your shadow.
                                                 Sing with sorrow.
                                                      Pray with joy.

                                 Each ending
                            empties summer.

                                                     We start again.

◆

                  There is a gate.
                They cannot return.

Her Wings

"What you see here, what you do here, what you hear here, when you leave here, let it stay here."

—The Manhattan Project, 1944

Ditch Flowers

You walk into a field
thinking:

> *a scorched cinder block
> is all love leaves.*

You once walked
through Jackson in the snow.
Your shoes filled with blood.
You crossed the Ohio line.
Got arrested.
Smiled anyway.
The cruiser was warm.

You follow broken singers
down 29 and 66,
roads wandered
by the hunted
and the hunters.
The hunting goes on.
No one stops the choir.

Mahalia Jackson's voice
was rust and root,
a kalbas drum
beating through ash.
We lost her.
She became a statue.

Suddenly, a girl
alone in a stone lot,
started singing.

The old woman named Joy,
who sang alto at Trinity Episcopal,
had a voice like a wire brush,
but she's gone now.
The church she sang in
was razed.
Now it's a field
off the Greene County line.

We're flames in the dark.
Building cemeteries in the middle of cities.
Apartments crowded in country fields.
Whistling past the wreckage.

Before the choir disappears,
I'll record them.

Turn them into ditch flowers,
growing heavy.

> *Hang wooden angels*
> *over checkerboard floors.*

I'll speak their names
so others know:

> *this river will not be broken.*

Notes

Angels Hung

The Wooden Angel is hung for my mother.
The Losing Kind is in memory of David A. Hill.
The Blew Light is for Mary Ann.
Ghosts Of The Bramble Slats is hung for Valerie.
To A Friend, Who After Being Diagnosed With Testicular Cancer Bought A Motorcycle To Race The Wind is in memory of the Cajun.
The Dark Flat Land is hung for my father.
Private Archipelago is in memory of Dan *PeeWeeToms* Thomas.
Mt. Washington Saturday Night is hung for Duke.
On Your Knees is for Michael Montgomery, Esq.
The Rain Horses is for Keith Sykes.
I Never Went To Saskatoon in memory of my dog, Chance.
The 18th Street Stairs is for my wife, Jessie.
A Road Map For 35 is for my daughter, Charlie, when she needs it.
Christmas In Budapest is hung for my brother, Joe, and in memory of his mother, Emma.
The Hard Swing is for David Melendez.

Acknowledgments

Grateful acknowledgment is made to the following publications, in which earlier forms of some of these poems originally appeared: *2River, Blind Man's Rainbow, The Brooklyner, Commonline Journal, Dunes Review, Foundling Review, I Had Cancer, King Log, Levitate Magazine, Lines + Stars, PulpMag, Poplorish, 491 Magazine, Stone Highway Review, The Rusty Nail, In the Teeth of the Wind, The Twin Cities Review, Turk's Head Review.*

A heartfelt thanks to **Marilynn Deane** and **Steve Pody**, who read this book in galleys and offered helpful notes.

Thanks also to the **Larry Levis Archives** at **Virginia Commonwealth University**, where I learned much about how to revise poems and where I was lucky enough to hold Larry's boots.

www.ingramcontent.com/pod-product-compliance
Lightning Source LLC
Chambersburg PA
CBHW030054170426
43197CB00010B/1524